# FRESH MANNA:

## INTRODUCTION TO THE STUDY
## OF GOD'S WORD

**Stan E. DeKoven, Ph.D.**

# FRESH MANNA:
## INTRODUCTION TO THE STUDY OF GOD´S WORD

## By Stan E. DeKoven, Ph.D.

Copyright © 1990 by Stan DeKoven
Second Edition 2012
ISBN 978-1-61529-068-0
For ordering information, please contact:

Vision Publishing
1672 Main St., E109
Ramona, CA 92065
1-800-9VISION (984-7466)
www.booksbyvision.com

# TABLE OF CONTENTS

# Forward

**Warning** -applying the principles for Bible study found in the book **FRESH MANNA: INTRODUCTION TO THE STUDY OF GOD´S WORD** will cause YOUR Bible to come alive and transform your life!

During my thirty-one years as a pastor and church planter in the United States and abroad I have learned the incredible value and importance of studying God's word. In my travels the one reoccurring question asked by new and seasoned believers in every country is, "How do I study the Bible?" The answer is found in this easy-to-understand book written by Dr. DeKoven revealing how to study the Bible through proven and effective Bible study methods.

In 2 Timothy 2:15, the Apostle Paul wrote, "Do your best to present yourself to God as one approved, a workman who does not need to be ashamed and who correctly handles the word of truth" (NIV). The Greek phrase translated "correctly handle" (*orthotomeo*) also means to "guide on a straight path." This book will help guide you on a straight path to the study and the simplicity of understanding God's word.

This book includes discussion on the authority and inspiration of Scripture, the importance of knowledge and understanding, the differences between the Old and New Testaments, and the importance of following divine authority instead of human authority. Also included is how to use study aids such as a bible concordance, various translations, and cross-references in an easy to understand way. This practical book will assist the student in starting an exciting journey of transformation and insight that is found only through proven and effective Bible study methods of God's word. Enjoy your journey!

Richard West Th.D./D. Min
Liberty Christian Center

# INTRODUCTION

My mother had quite an influence on me. As a young boy, my mom and dad would send us to the local Sunday school. We first learned about Jesus there. I am convinced that their motivation for sending us was mixed; a combination of wanting us to have some solid moral instruction, and an opportunity to have some private time together.

When President John F. Kennedy was assassinated, that all changed. Her world of security had been shattered, and her broken heart was turned towards God. In her own inimitable way, she had to have Christ. She went to church and gave her heart to the Lord, and her life, in spite of the normal stresses of life, was never the same....and the rest of family soon followed suit, giving our hearts to Jesus as well.

My mom was far from perfect of course...but she did love the Word of God; especially the Amplified Bible. I think she liked it because she liked to read, and having more words must mean it was more spiritual. Every morning when she would get up, usually very early, before any of the rest of us, she would start the coffee, pour herself a cup, pull out her bible and the "Daily Bread", light up a cigarette, and enjoy time with Jesus. Like I said, she wasn't perfect, but devoted she was, and she learned the important things in the word of God; about loving a neighbor, helping a friend, caring for her family, being faithful in relationships, serving in the sometimes crazy institution called the church. In other words, she grew, and grew up, as she studied the word of God and acted upon it...not without struggle, but I am certain her life was pleasing to God.

Success in our spiritual life can be best defined as faithfulness over time...faithful in time, talent and treasure, faithful in our devotion and discipline to the Lord, faithful in service in the areas of gifting or the calling we have, whatever that may be.

Fresh Manna is not a comprehensive book on hermeneutics; it is an introductory text, with a specific design to whet the appetite of the reader to desire to read and study the word of God for the rest of their life. As a lifelong learner, one who is enamored with the Book of all Books, my prayer is that the helps provided will inspire the student to dig out the nuggets of truth, and fall more and more in love with the Lord of the Book....Jesus.

Dr Stan DeKoven

2012

# CHAPTER I:

# STUDYING GOD'S WORD

Over the past several years a number of Christian leaders have fallen from grace. The reasons for their fall are numerous, and the laity has been hurt because of their fall. In many cases, the sheep have fallen away because their eyes were on the man or woman of God and not on the Lord Jesus Christ as revealed through His Word.

A burning concern of most Christian leaders is to see their congregational members learn to study God's Word in an effective and systematic fashion. Most Christians **read** the Word, some study it for a certain purpose (like writing a Bible College paper), but few truly study in a **systematic fashion.**

In order to grow deeper in the things of God, and to insure that one will stand in the day of temptation, the Christian must have **knowledge** and **wisdom.** Knowledge comes from reading and meditating on the Word of God. Wisdom is the application of God's Word to the individual's life.

If there is reverence (fear) for the Lord, there will be a seeking of these attitudes and a desire to grow in them.

## BIBLE STUDY

Several years ago the Rev. Bruce Wingard, M.Div. developed a note-taking system called the WordWise Bible Study System. This program allows a student of the Word to take notes on special paper right in his/her Bible. Along with Wingard's system (unfortunately, no longer available) was provided a small guide that offers some helpful hints called the **14 Fundamentals of Bible Study.** Twelve of his steps and other helps used over the past few years by this writer are included in this book to assist the student in a systematic study of God's Word. But first things first.

## WHY STUDY?

Psalm 119, verse 105 states,

> *"Your word is a lamp to my feet and a light to my path."*

Christians need a light before them to guide them through life's difficult paths. Like the high-beams on a car, the Word of God illuminates the mind and heart and shows the "Way, Truth, and Life." Jesus is the living Word, which became flesh and lived among men (John 1:1), and the Bible is the living Word of God for man. God's Word:

| *Guides | *Inspires | *Strengthens | *Directs |
|---|---|---|---|

*Teaches  *Instructs  *Causes good works

*Trains in righteousness  *Corrects  *Equips

(2 Timothy 3:16, 17)

**There are several reasons why we need to study God's Word, they include:**

1.  The power of God's Word, when received in the hearts of men, by the anointing of the Holy Spirit, brings the knowledge of sin and the need for repentance. It further brings salvation in Jesus through believing on His Name.

2.  The study of the Word brings growth in Christ. Like any good mother or father, God the Father wants us to grow to maturity. To grow, we must learn principles of truth to be aptly applied so that we might be transformed (Romans 12:2).

    *"And do not be conformed to this world: but be transformed by the renewing of your mind, that you*

*may prove what the will of God is, that which is good and acceptable and perfect."*

3. The Word will help in times of trouble, give strength in trials, give focus and purpose for life, and demonstrate how God deals with his children to bring about their good.

   *"And we know that God causes all things to work together for good to those who love God, to those who are called according to His purpose." (Romans 8:28)*

Before reviewing the steps to effective private study of God's Word, it would be helpful to understand the "word" being discussed.

## WORDS FOR THE "WORD"

In the Greek, there are three basic words used for our one word "word". They are: *GRAPHE, LOGOS, and RHEMA.* These three words together give the student a complete picture of God's plan for the study of the Word of God.

# GRAPHE

The *Graphe* is the written Word of God (2 Timothy 3:16-17).

*"All scripture (word, graphe) is given by inspiration of God, and is profitable for teaching, for reproof, for correction, for training in righteousness, so that the man of God may be adequate, equipped for every good work."*

The Bible, regardless of the version, is the authoritative and complete revelation of God's plan and purpose for mankind. Within the Bible God's complete revelation of salvation can be found, culminating in Jesus Christ. Reading and studying of the *graphe* is essential to "life and godliness".

## LOGOS

The *Logos* of God is the incarnate Word, or the Word made Flesh (also called the Living Word, the Bread of Life, etc.). Jesus Christ is the Living Word or *Logos*, which according to Hebrews 4:12 is even more powerful than the *Rhema* of God, or a word from God.

> *"For the word of God is living and active and sharper than any two-edged sword, and piercing as far as the division of soul and spirit, of both joints and marrow, and able to judge the thoughts and intentions of the heart."*

As a believer, a man receives the *Logos* or Word made flesh through confession and belief (Romans 10:9,10), at which point man receives salvation.

> *" ...that if you confess with your mouth Jesus as Lord, and believe in your heart that God raised Him from the dead, you will be saved; for with the heart a person believes, resulting in righteousness, and with the mouth he confesses, resulting in salvation."*

## RHEMA

As stated briefly above, a *Rhema* is a specific word from the Lord for individual believers. This **word** releases faith to take action. Often, the Holy Spirit will speak to Christians of the Living Word (*logos*) through the written word (*graphe*) which will provide a revealed word (*rhema*) to give guidance or release power. All three of the different manifestations of the Word are necessary and available for the believing Christian.

## Questions for Thought and Discussion

1.  Discuss some of the reasons for studying God's Word

2.  Look up the words *graphe, logos and rhema* in the Strong's concordance and write out the definition found there:

    Graphe

    Logos

    Rhema

3.  What is the most important quality of good study?

4.  What two things must the Christian have in the times in which we live?  KNOWLEDGE & WISDOM

5.  Describe your typical Bible study time.

6. Record below any personal observations or insights gained through the reading of Chapter I.

## CHAPTER II:

## THE FUNDAMENTALS

The following fundamentals will prove to be of great value to the student of the Word of God. Like any system of learning or study, the fundamentals are only as good as the effort of the student using them. Knowing the fundamentals, but not practicing them, is much like reading the Word of God and not acting according to the teachings of the Word. At the end of this chapter there will be a listing of all of the fundamentals dealt with here. The student should make a copy of the rules and keep them before him whenever studying.

## 1. USE THE RIGHT BIBLE

Many students ask, "Which study Bible is the best?" There are so many to choose from, and more are coming on the market every year. The following suggestions are only the opinion of this writer, but represent the Bibles that have been the most helpful in study.

Many people prefer the King James Version of the Bible, because it is the version that they were raised with. There are still a few hold-outs who will insist that it is not spiritual to even think of using another version. Later in this book, in the chapter on the **Tools of Study,** some of the weaknesses in the King James Version are presented: weaknesses that have been corrected in the New King James Version.

Along with the New King James Version there are several other newer translations or versions available. The New International Version (NIV) is fast becoming the preferred version of many Christians (especially ministers).

The NIV is recommended for new converts, especially because of the clarity of language. My dear friend and theologian, Dr. Ken Chant added the following; "The NIV is good, but the more recent English Standard Version (ESV) is better. It displays less evangelical bias, is more accurate, and generally reads better from the pulpit. I like the NIV, but one cannot deny that when the translators were faced with a choice between the biblical text and proper evangelical dogma the dogma always won! The New American Standard Bible is good, too, but it reads heavily, and the translation principle of always rendering a Greek or Hebrew verb in the same way in English makes neither a truly reliable translation nor for smooth reading."

The New American Standard Bible is a personal favorite, as it is a translation that is very close to the original biblical languages. I often joke that the reason I prefer this book is obvious in the name…it is new, it is American, and it is the standard! Of course, no version is absolutely perfect in all aspects. This is true for many reasons that are beyond the scope of this book. For more information on how we obtained our modern Bible, it is recommended that the student obtain Dr. Ken Chant's book, "The Bible", and for a more thorough understanding of the interpretation of the Bible, Dr. Chant's book "Understanding the Bible". Both are available from Vision Publishing.

The serious student of the Bible should choose a Bible with a good concordance in the back. In the chapter on **Tools of Study** a complete concordance will be recommended, but it is nice to have a shorter version in the back of one's Bible so that scriptures can be found at times when the student is not at the normal place of study.

Another consideration is the size of print and the size of the Bible. It goes without saying that the larger the print the larger the Bible. Many new converts are tricked into buying a large "family sized Bible" by some smooth talking Bible salesman. The problem is that after a short while they realize that the Bible is much too large and heavy to carry and it simply collects dust on an end table.

A personal Bible should be large enough to have print that is easily read and with a concordance, but the Bible should be small enough to be carried comfortably at any time. It is also advisable to have a Bible large enough to carry some notes in, etc. The important thing is to have a usable Bible, or better yet, as will be discussed later, several different translations or versions to be used in making comparisons and to enrich study.

Although many Christian prefer a leather covered Bible, the extra editions to be used for study purposes need not be leather bound because of the high cost of leather binding. In some cases a paper bound issue of some version will serve the student quite well.

For those students with internet access, an excellent resource may be found at www.biblegateway.com. Many different translations are found there as well as versions in languages other than English.

## 2. DEVELOP GOOD STUDY HABITS

The most difficult part of studying anything is getting started. Many people have not learned adequate study skills in their early academic experiences, and have developed an aversion to studying. Truly, studying is work! Yet, God's Word is clear. Christians must study (be diligent) to show themselves approved unto God. (2 Timothy 2:15) *"Be diligent to present yourself approved to God as a workman who does not need to be ashamed, accurately handling the word of truth."*

Meditating on God's Word means to set as a priority time with the Lord and his Word. The importance of time with God and his Word cannot be overemphasized for the development of spiritual vitality.

Good, God-pleasing study habits will begin with establishing a separate place for study. This should be a place which is reasonably quiet (many people like soft worship music playing when they study), free of common distractions, such as kids, phones, neighbors or a needy spouse. It may not be possible to get rid of all distractions, but an effort must be made to limit them as much as possible. It is advisable to find and make sacred a place of study that can be used solely for that purpose.

The place of study should be reasonably warm or comfortably cool. No place may be perfect.

It is also important to have the necessary study aids (concordance, dictionary, computer, etc.) at ready access. Spending precious time chasing down study materials can be frustrating, at best. Satan will do everything in his power to distract the true student of the Word. He is easily defeated by will power and determination, along with a steady dose of the Word of God.

It is vital to maintain a relaxed and normal internal (inside ones body) environment while studying. Having a cup of coffee or a snack while studying is fine, but it is advisable to make sure that the coffee and/or snack are readily available. It is amazing how distracting a missing cup of coffee can be.

The whole idea is for the student to be as comfortable as possible. Studying should not create discomfort or anxiety. Studying God's Word can and should be a most enjoyable and thoroughly profitable activity. The more something is enjoyed the more the student is likely to continue this positive and beneficial behavior.

Finally, it is advisable to set a specific period of time for studying. It is highly recommended that one study at the same time every day for about the same period of time. The discipline of setting time limits will go a long way in making the student faithful in studying and in other endeavors for the Lord. However, one should not become overly rigid or obsessed if a schedule cannot be met perfectly. Life is filled with many variables, and flexibility is a sign of maturity, as long as it is not used as an excuse to avoid responsibility.

## 3. PREPARE THE HEART

In the Book of Ezra 7:10 it is recorded,

> *"For Ezra had set his heart to study the law of the Lord and to practice it, and to teach His statutes and ordinances in Israel."*

There are many things that the Christians can "set" their hearts upon, many of which are good and wholesome. When talking about the study of God's Word, preparation of the heart is vital.

If individuals expect to accomplish anything for the Lord, and become effective in service for him, they must set their hearts to study God's Word. To accomplish this, the following recommendation is by far the most helpful:

Quiet the heart. God encourages us in Psalm 46:10 to

> *"Cease striving and know that I am God; I will be exalted among the nations, I will be exalted in the earth."*

That is, God's desire is for his children to quiet their hearts and minds from needless and futile worry. Taking a few deep breaths and closing the eyes can be most relaxing. Relaxation is not easy for people with obsessive thoughts or overly perfectionistic intentions. However, with practice and God's help almost anyone can accomplish this important spiritual step.

## 4. CONFESS THE WORD

Confession in this context does not mean that if something is said over and over, even God's Word, that automatically what is being repeated will come to pass, and that every fantasy of will must be fulfilled by the Lord. The truth of God's Word will set a person free, but only if they abide in or continue in his Word.

> *"If you continue in my word, then you are truly disciples of Mine."* (John 8:31)

Further, confession is not just talking without action. It is imperative to be doers as well as hearers.

> *"But prove yourselves doers of the word, and not merely hearers who delude themselves." (James 1:22)*

What is the importance of confession or speaking the Word? Firstly, confession and believing the Word brings salvation.

> *"...if you confess with your mouth Jesus as Lord, and believe in your heart that God raised Him from the dead, you will be saved." (Romans 10:9)*

Second, Christians are to confess Christ if they are truly his disciples.

> "And I say to you, everyone who confesses Me before men, the Son of Man will confess him also before the angels of God. *" (Luke 12:8)*

Third, believers are to confess the Lordship of Jesus, his preeminence over all things.

> *"And that every tongue should confess that Jesus Christ is Lord, to the glory of God the Father."* (Philippians 2:11)

Fourth, in the life of the Christian, when sin is recognized, we are to confess to experience God's forgiveness (which has already been granted through Christ).

> *"If we confess our sins, he is faithful and just to forgive us our sins, and to cleanse us from all unrighteousness." (1 John 1:9)*

Fifth, praying the Word is a form of confession, and brings the believer into intimate relationship with the Lord. Further, through the praying of the Word of God, when understood in proper context it can bring us into agreement with the will and purpose of the Lord and bring into reality the focus of our prayers.

Finally, Christians must confess or speak the truth of God's Word to overcome the lies of the flesh or the enemy.

> *"For the word of God is living and active and sharper than any two-edged sword, and piercing as far as the division of soul and spirit, of both joints and marrow, and able to judge the thoughts and intentions of the heart." (Hebrews 4:12)*

Also,

> *"For the weapons of our warfare are not of the flesh, but divinely powerful for the destruction of fortresses. We are destroying speculations and every lofty thing raised up against the knowledge of God, and we are taking every thought captive to the obedience of Christ, and we are ready to punish all disobedience, whenever your obedience is complete." (2 Corinthians 10:4-6)*

Through confessing the Word of God and abiding in his Word one will see:

- **Salvation and Deliverance**
- **Healing and Restoration**
- **Strength and Power**
- **Comfort and Assurance**

All that the Christian needs to grow in God's grace and knowledge of the Lord is to be found in God's Word.

## 5. TAKE AUTHORITY OVER THE ENEMY: COOPERATE WITH THE HOLY SPIRIT

The fact is, once a person is "in Christ", he is a new creation.

> *"Therefore if anyone is in Christ, he is a new creature; the old things passed away; behold, new things have come." (2 Corinthians 5:17)*

The Christian has been translated from the kingdom of darkness to the Kingdom of his own dear Son, becoming bathed in the light of God's love. However, there is still a need to live in the physical realm, and all Christians are subject to trials and temptations, and have strengths and weaknesses. Satan knows that he cannot possess the Christian's spirit and that the Christian is lost to the kingdom of darkness. Therefore, Satan's strategy in the believer's life is to render him powerless, leaving him feeling condemned and defeated, and inhibiting him from reaching his potential in Christ. Satan may have lost the Christian to the Kingdom of God, but he continues to fight to keep him from bringing others into Christ' Kingdom.

> *"For our struggle is not against flesh and blood, but against the rulers, against the powers, against the world forces of this darkness, against the spiritual forces of wickedness in the heavenly places." (Ephesians 6:12)*

An ignorant Christian is a powerless Christian. One who does not pray or study God's precious Word, will be ineffective. Therefore, when a believer purposes in his/her heart to study the Word and pray, there will always be opposition.

We know that the enemy was defeated by Christ through His death on the cross,

> *"Therefore, since the children share in flesh and blood, He Himself likewise also partook of the same, that through death He might render powerless him who had the power of death, that is, the devil," (Hebrews 2:14)*

The Christian has been given the authority to command Satan in Christ's name

*"And Jesus came up and spoke to them, saying, "All authority has been given to Me in heaven and on earth. Go therefore and make disciples of all the nations, baptizing them in the name of the Father and the Son and the Holy Spirit," (Matthew 28:18-19).*

Note also,

*"These signs will accompany those who have believed: in My name they will cast out demons, they will speak with new tongues;" (Mark 16:17)*

Christians are further commanded to resist the devil after they have submitted themselves totally to the Lord.

*...do not give the devil an opportunity." (Ephesians 4:27).*

Also,

*"Put on the full armor of God, so that you will be able to stand firm against the schemes of the devil." (Ephesians 6:11).*

And,

*"Submit therefore to God. Resist the devil and he will flee from you." (James 4:7)*

Finally,

*"Be of sober spirit, be on the alert. Your adversary, the devil, prowls around like a roaring lion, seeking someone to devour." (I Peter 5: 8)*

A careful study of the above scriptures will show that even though the devil has been bound and defeated by Christ, the Christian must daily recognize his strategies and prepare himself for the attacks. The believer must exercise his God given authority whenever preparing to study the Word of God.

In Matthew 18:18 it is recorded that whatever a Christian binds on earth is bound in heaven and whatever the believer looses on earth is also loosed in heaven. The Christian believer must take their authority, submit to the Lord and openly resist the devil in their attempts to hinder the study of God's Word and the believer's growth in God.

Satan will use many different forms of distraction, he will:

- **Cause the mind to wander**
- **Create false emergencies**
- **Get the children into trouble**
- **Cause weariness (fatigue)**

The Christian must ask the Holy Spirit to minister to him through the Word. It is the Holy Spirit who comforts, leads into truth, convicts of sin, fills the believer, brings fruit into the believer's life, and ultimately is the teacher and guide. Christians need the Holy Spirit to be released in their lives that they might continue to grow in God.

## 6. DON'T GET SIDE-TRACKED

As mentioned in point 5 above, the devil would like to distract the child of God from the important task of studying God's Word. The Christian must resist the devil in the Spirit, and become a good steward of time and circumstances. One way to learn stewardship of God's time is by keeping oneself on track, moving in a specific direction for a primary purpose.

One of the things that the Army tries to teach its officers is the importance of paying attention to detail. Officers are taught to focus their mental energies on seeing a task through to completion. In spite of possible obstacles, the main mission (in the case of the Christian, studying God's Word systematically) is always what matters.

In this present age, the average attention span of an adult is less than 15 minutes. Attention to detail or staying on task is virtually a lost art. Yet, when a person considers that the reading of God's word is part of communion with the God of the universe, those who truly love God and realize how much he loves them will find it less difficult to attend to the task or rather, will find the joy of studying the Words of their Father.

Some practical hints might be helpful to the student in his studies:

- Stay consistent with a schedule. Where possible, study at the same time and place every day.

- Remove as many distractions as possible to include taking the phone off the hook or leaving the answering machine on.

- Should the mind begin to wander, it is best not to condemn oneself but to simply return to the task.

- The quality of relationship is much more important than the quantity of study. It is important to read the Word and pray until the Lord ministers the truth to the heart. It is much like eating several small meals instead of one very large one.

- The wise student of the Word does not skip around in his reading but remains steadfast in their resolve to systematically learn of the Lord.

- As the student learns to trust the Lord he will realize that the Lord will help him study more effectively and thoroughly. God has invested his best in each Christian and he will guard over his investment.

## 7. READ TO SOMEONE ELSE OUT LOUD AND/OR LISTEN WHILE THEY READ TO YOU

Many adults can remember the joy of listening to a teacher read to them in the first few grades in school. Teachers say that the times that they have the least problems with discipline or restlessness on the part of their children are when they read to them in class. People love to be read to.

Reading to someone else, or listening to someone read the Word of God (while following along in the text) will allow the Holy Spirit to speak even more clearly. Listening to an audio tape of someone reading the Bible can help the student concentrate more effectively. Reading the Word aloud can also be an opportunity for ministry, as someone else might be listening.

## 8. DISCUSS WITH SOMEONE WHAT YOU ARE READING AND WHAT THE HOLY SPIRIT IS TEACHING YOU

The Holy Spirit desires to bring God's people into deeper truth.

> *"As for you, the anointing which you received from Him abides in you, and you have no need for anyone to teach you; but as His anointing teaches you about all things, and is true and is not a lie, and just as it has taught you, you abide in Him." (1 John 2:27)*

> *"I will ask the Father, and He will give you another Helper, that He may be with you forever." (John 14:16)*

> *"But the Helper, the Holy Spirit, whom the Father will send in My name, He will teach you all things, and bring to your remembrance all that I said to you." (John 14: 26)*

When Christians discuss the Word of God with other believers, especially those who are more mature in the Lord, they can gain new insights and perceptions that they did not formerly have. Further, this is often the sweetest form of Christian fellowship, as together they bless each other through a discussion of the Word.

In Luke 24:44-46, Luke says,

> *"Now He said to them, "These are My words which I spoke to you while I was still with you, that all things which are written about Me in the Law of Moses and the Prophets and the Psalms must be fulfilled." Then He opened their minds to understand the Scriptures, and He said to them, "Thus it is written, that the Christ would suffer and rise again from the dead the third day."*

In this passage, Jesus was sharing openly with His disciples about what was to take place after his resurrection and about the outpouring of the Holy Spirit. Jesus makes the revelational statement that he himself is the Living Word. The 45th verse states that he "opened their minds, to understand the scriptures." As Christians discuss the Word of God, when two or three are gathered in Jesus Name, understanding will be opened and the Holy Spirit will speak. All Christians need to understand God's Word, which most often occurs through the discussion of the truths of the Bible as revealed by the Holy Spirit through each believer.

## 9. RECEIVE THE WORD WITH AN OPEN AND SUBMITTED HEART

There is no substitute for submission to the Lord and obedience to his Word. An open and submitted heart could best be illustrated by the life of Mary,

> *"She (Martha) had a sister called Mary, who was seated at the Lord's feet, listening to His word."*
> *(Luke 10:39)*

It was at the feet of Jesus that Mary was taught God's Word. She also ministered to the Lord through her acts of worship and obedience.

A person with an open heart is one that will ask God the Holy Spirit to reveal truth about ones life. Further, this person will diligently pray that the Word of God will begin to renew their mind.

> *"Therefore I urge you, brethren, by the mercies of God, to present your bodies a living and holy sacrifice, acceptable to God, which is your spiritual service of worship. And do not be conformed to this world, but be transformed by the renewing of your mind, so that you may prove what the will of God is, that which is good and acceptable and perfect."*

(Romans 12:1-2)

The scripture also states that God desires His children to be conformed to the image of Christ.

> *"...and have put on the new self who is being renewed to a true knowledge according to the image of the One who created him." (Colossians 3:10)*

That is, each believer's highest good and purpose can only be fulfilled through Christ in them, the hope of glory.

Along with submission to the Lord, his children are to be submitted to all legitimate authority, especially to their spiritual leaders in the local church.

> *"Obey your leaders and submit to them, for they keep watch over your souls as those who will give an account. Let them do this with joy and not with grief, for this would be unprofitable for you." (Hebrews 13:17)*

As the student receives the Word and acts on it, his attitude towards himself and others will begin to change. The student's ability to love (Agape) will grow, and his sensitivity to hear God's voice will increase. The Lord desires that his children grow in his grace and in the knowledge of him.

*"...but grow in the grace and knowledge of our Lord and Savior Jesus Christ. To Him be the glory, both now and to the day of eternity. Amen."* (2 Peter 3:18)

## 10. READ SYSTEMATICALLY UNDER THE HOLY SPIRIT'S GUIDANCE, AND BE ALERT TO WHAT HE WILL TEACH YOU

It is advisable to instruct a new convert to begin reading the Bible in the Gospel of St. John. From there they should read I John, then the other gospels, the Pauline epistles, the General epistles. They should be taught to read a Psalm and one of the Proverbs every day. Later they may work their way through the Old Testament.

This simple program of study seems effective for older Christians as well as new converts, because it is a systematic form of study. The Lord may, however, direct an individual in a different manner. The student must always be sensitive to the leading of the Lord.

A systematic reading and study of God's Word, and an openness of heart to the Lord's direction will build a foundation for further growth in Christian living. There are some cautions that should be considered. These include:

- Remember, the Holy Spirit is in charge. He knows the needs of people, and therefore should be consulted before pushing ahead.

- It is always helpful in a systematic study for it to be supervised, through discussion with a more mature believer. This will insure that:

    - The Word was actually read (accountability and discipline is established.)

    - The understanding of the Word is clear.

    - Questions can be adequately answered.

    - Doctrinal error can be avoided.

- The goal of study, especially at the beginning, is to become progressively intimate with Jesus. Reading in St. John and in 1 John will lead the believer into a more intimate relationship with Christ.

The systematic study of God's Word, followed by systematic teaching (see the bibliography for recommended teaching tools) and through other study helps, will ensure that a firm foundation is built under the feet of the believer.

## 11. RECORD INSIGHTS, IDEAS AND QUESTIONS

The Word of God will bring new insights, ideas and questions to mind as the Bible is systematically read. These insights should be recorded in a journal.

The prophet Habakkuk was instructed by the Lord to

> *"write the vision and make it plain upon tables, that he may run that readeth it."* (Habakkuk. 2:2, KJV)

That is excellent advice for Christians today. As the Lord begins to speak, the student of the Word should write down and share with others the words and ideas that the Lord gives. Listed below are a few suggestions on how to journal:

- Although any notebook will do, some people find that a loose-leaf notebook has some advantages.

- The Student should either carry the notebook with him or figure out a way to keep notes safe, to be later transferred to the study notebook.

- As the Holy Spirit gives special thoughts, insights or questions they should be recorded in the notebook with the date, time of day and circumstance.

- The student's insights should be shared with someone they love and trust. Ideas could be shared with a friend, while questions could be shared with either the pastor or an elder.

Many times a student will be an instrument to bring a Word from the Lord to someone that is in need.

The sharing of insights with mature leadership provides necessary protection from possible error. In 2 Peter 1:20 the Apostle Peter provides a warning to the church that no prophecy, or "Word of the Lord", is of one's own private interpretation. Only in the counsel of mature believers can the Christian be certain that an insight is accurate or that an idea should be implemented. As in any endeavor, the more one practices a certain skill, the better he will become at the skill. One must learn to trust the Lord to help record the visions, etc., that the Lord may give, and be open enough to share with others and receive correction as needed. Only the Lord is perfect, and thus all believers (yes, even Pastors) can make mistakes. That is why the Lord called all into a Body, and likens the Christian to a family. We need each other!

In Chapter V of this text (Study Helps), the student will find several sample forms that can be duplicated to make the whole business of recording information a lot easier.

## 12. TERMINATE THE STUDY GUILT FREE AT THE HOLY SPIRIT'S DIRECTION.

One of the primary tricks of the devil is to attempt to bring condemnation, which leads to guilt and legalistic bondage. Romans 8:1 says,

> *"Therefore there is now no condemnation for those which are in Christ Jesus."*

When the Christian sits down to study God's word, it is like dining with a special friend. When dining, the food (God's Word) should be enjoyed, and the diners should eat until they are satisfied. Eating too little will leave a person hungry, while eating too much will cause a person to feel painfully over stuffed and lethargic.

When the Christian reads the Word and takes time for praise, worship and prayer it is wise to leave the study table slightly hungry. That slight hunger will give the seeker a desire to come again and enjoy yet another delicious meal with Christ. It is important to remember that <u>although food is important to health, strength and restoration, the relationship with the Friend is most vital.</u> Remember, we are seated in the heavenlies with Christ, so, it is as though the Christian is sitting in "heavenly places" when he reads the Word and communes with the greatest friend of all, one who is closer than a brother. It is this Brother who loves with an eternal love and desires to have fellowship with his children. No one needs fear to come to the table, nor should they fear leaving it when full. The Father loves the sweet fellowship of his children gathering at the table he has prepared.

**Copy this list and place it some place in your study so you can see it. This will help you remember.**

- Use the right Bible.

- Develop good study habits.

- Prepare the heart.

- Confess the Word concerning the scriptures.

- Take your authority over the devil and ask Holy Spirit to minister to you.

- Do not get side-tracked.

- Read to someone else/listen to someone else read.

- Discuss with someone what you have read and what Holy Spirit is teaching you.

- Receive the Word with an open and submitted heart.

- Read systematically under the Holy Spirit's guidance; be alert to what you read.

- Record insights, ideas and questions.

- Terminate the study time guilt free.

## Questions for Discussion and Thought

1. Which two of the 12 suggestions above seem to be the most important for you?  Why?

   *RECORD INSIGHTS. I OFTEN HAVE FLOODS OF THOUGHTS*
   (*A* inserted above)

2. Which two might be the most difficult for you to implement?

   *TAKE YOUR AUTH OVER DEVIL — I DON'T OFTEN ACKNOWLEDGE MY STRUGGLES AS COMING FROM OUTSIDE ME*

   *DO NOT GET SIDETRACKED*

3. Which Bible do you prefer to use?  Why?

   *NIV — READS EASY & MOST OF THE PHRASES ARE CONSISTENT ITS NOT PERFECT BUT IT WORKS.*
   *OR NAS. I KNOW ITS MORE ACCURATE BUT I DON'T FIND IT READS AS EASY AS NIV.*

4. What study habits do you need to work on?

   *Don't KNOW, PROBABLY PRAYING & DECLARING MORE THEN STUDYING*

5. What is meant by preparing one's heart for study?

   *BE OPEN FOR HOLY SPIRIT TO CLEAN HOUSE OR REPENTANCE.*

6. How can the student avoid getting sidetracked during study?

*STUDY WHEN THERE ISN'T AS MUCH TO GET SIDETRACKED BY*

7. What does the author mean by systematic study?

*STUDY WITH INTENTION & SYSTEM*

8. Why should the student record insights, ideas and questions?

*UNRECORDED INSIGHTS GET LOST & MOST INSIGHTS ARE OFTEN FOR A LATER USE.*

9. Record below any personal observations or insights gained through the reading of Chapter II.

*GOOD BASIC REMINDERS OF PRACTICAL OBSTICALS PEOPLE FACE. ALSO MAKES ME THINK THIS WOULD BE ESPECIALLY USEFUL IN OTHER COUNTRIES.*

## *CHAPTER III:*

# HERMENEUTICS[1]

*"Hermeneutics"* is a word from the Greek that means to "explain" or "interpret". The Bible student's task then, is to follow established rules that will help him to read the scriptures responsibly, and to interpret them well and wisely.

## RULES FOR UNDERSTANDING THE BIBLE

### YOU CAN UNDERSTAND THE BIBLE

The Bible can, and should, be read like any other book: it uses ordinary language, and its words carry their ordinary meanings. There are times when certain words will need to be researched because of the changes in meaning that may have occurred. The message of the Bible can be taken at face value, and acted upon without further influence being necessary.

> *"For this commandment which I command you today is not too difficult for you, nor is it out of reach. It is not in heaven, that you should say, 'Who will go up to heaven for us to get it for us and make us hear it, that we may observe it?' Nor is it beyond the sea, that you should say, 'Who will cross the sea for us to get it for us and make us hear it, that we may observe it?' But the word is very near you, in your mouth and in your heart, that you may observe it." (Deuteronomy 30:11-14)*

**All reliable Bible study begins at this point: simply read; believe what you read; and act upon it!**

---

[1] The author wishes to thank Dr. Ken Chant for providing the basis of the material in this chapter.

Failure to observe this rule can lead to foolish interpretations; See Proverbs 30:4,

> *"Who has ascended into heaven and descended? Who has gathered the wind in His fists? Who has wrapped the waters in His garment? Who has established all the ends of*
>
> *the earth? What is His name or His son's name? Surely you know!"*

However, while the Bible can be understood, many people fail to understand it. Why would that be?

## THE BIBLE CAN BE MISUNDERSTOOD

Many warnings are given against mishandling the word of God:

> *"Remind them of these things, and solemnly charge them in the presence of God not to wrangle about words, which is useless and leads to the ruin of the hearers. Be diligent to present yourself approved to God as a workman who does not need to be ashamed, accurately handling the word of truth. But avoid worldly and empty chatter, for it will lead to further ungodliness, and their talk will spread like gangrene. Among them are Hymenaeus and Philetus, men who have gone astray from the truth saying that the resurrection has already taken place, and they upset the faith of some." (2 Timothy 2:14-18)*
>
> *Jesus said to them, "Is this not the reason you are mistaken, that you do not understand the Scriptures or the power of God?" (Mark 12:24)*
>
> *"...as also in all his letters, speaking in them of these things, in which are some things hard to understand, which the untaught and unstable*

*distort, as they do also the rest of the Scriptures, to their own destruction." (2 Peter 3:16)*

*For we are not like many, peddling the word of God, but as from sincerity, but as from God, we speak in Christ in the sight of God." (2 Corinthians 2:17)*

Not even sincerity, prayer, or fasting can provide adequate protection against error if wrong principles of interpretation are followed. There are many erroneous books where authors base their certainty upon much prayer and/or fasting, instead of study.

## Why is this so?

Because we are separated from the biblical authors, by at least 2000 years:

### 1. Historically

This gap is difficult to cross; we are prone to think wrongly that the writer of Holy Writ was the same as we are. It is true that Elijah was a man just as we are; subject to the same passions, but because of the differences in culture and historical background there is a significant difference between the perceptions and understandings of the writers of the Bible from modern man.

### 2. Culturally

The authors of the bible, though inspired by the Holy Spirit, had a significantly different lifestyles, different social relationships between men and women, adults and children, rulers and subjects, etc.

Imagine a world without books, little music, magical medicine (there was little medical research, because disease was thought to come either from demons or God).

There is no Hebrew word for "family", they spoke instead of the "household".

There is no Hebrew word for "marriage"; they saw the event only as a contract arranged by two fathers or guardians; the girl usually had no say in the matter.

No doubt many men loved their wives, as Boaz loved Ruth; but he loved her as a precious possession, not as a friend or partner; hence Ruth placed herself at his feet, acknowledging him as her lord. There was no place in the culture for the kind of conjugal love that is our ideal. For example: Daughters could be sold as concubines.

> *"If a man sells his daughter as a female slave, she is not to go free as the male slaves do. If she is displeasing in the eyes of her master who designated her for himself, then he shall let her be redeemed. He does not have authority to sell her to a foreign people because of his unfairness to her. If he designates her for his son, he shall deal with her according to the custom of daughters. If he takes to himself another woman, he may not reduce her food, her clothing, or her conjugal rights. If he will not do these three things for her, then she shall go out for nothing, without payment of money."* *(Exodus 21:7-11)*

> *See Lot offering his daughters.*

> *But Lot went out to them at the doorway, and shut the door behind him, and said, "Please, my brothers, do not act wickedly. Now behold, I have two daughters who have not had relations with man; please let me bring them out to you, and do to them whatever you like; only do nothing to these men, inasmuch as they have come under the shelter of my roof."* *(Genesis 19:6-8)*

See Moses' peculiar test of conjugal fidelity, laid upon women only, not men.

*"...and this water that brings a curse shall go into your stomach, and make your abdomen swell and your thigh waste away." And the woman shall say, "Amen. Amen." 'The priest shall then write these curses on a scroll, and he shall wash them off into the water of bitterness. Then he shall make the woman drink the water of bitterness that brings a curse, so that the water which brings a curse will go into her and cause bitterness."*

(Numbers 5:22-24)

Notice that the daily labor of all the people, both men and women, was long and hard.

### 3. Linguistically

Note their use of exaggeration, such as in the curse formulae, etc. Many of the stories and proverbs make use of idioms. One of the problems with idioms is that they tend to change their meaning from one generation to another. Idioms represent the most complex part of a language. Consider the idiom in English, "Saved by the skin of our teeth." Foreigners would have trouble understanding the meaning of such an idiom. During the failed coup in Russia in August of 1991, a Russian diplomat was heard to misuse an American idiom. He said that the people had, "the over hand" in the situation, instead of the "upper hand." The full meaning of many Old Testament words seem uncertain, requiring caution before making a dogmatic interpretation of a word or phrase.

### 4. Philosophically

The worldview of the writers of the Old and New Testaments was vastly different from the worldview of people in the 21st century. The fact that there were great philosophical differences between people of the Bible period and those who translated the earliest manuscripts should be taken into account when studying the Bible.

In particular, the Hebrews saw God in everything:

- in drought, locusts, etc.

- God was reckoned to have brought every invader into the land (see Isaiah 45:1-7)

- houses were thought to contract leprosy (Leviticus 13:33 ff.)

- they had no scruples about genocide (Numbers 31:7,15-17). This is a passage that both Catholics and Protestants used to justify murdering each other!

## 5. Spiritually

Twenty plus centuries of Christian history and theology may not have made us any better, but they have certainly made us different!

**Those five distinctions lead to three principles -**

- It must be recognized that the Bible was not originally written for 21st century English speaking Christians, but for ancient people far removed from us in culture, attitude, and understanding. The Holy Spirit necessarily permitted the book to be written in terms that would be meaningful and acceptable to those people.

- This applies to the whole Bible, not just to those parts that are difficult or obviously obsolete (like the bitter water of jealousy); one cannot just remove the obviously objectionable parts, and then read the remainder as though it had been written last week.

- The entire book must be read as an ancient document, and the question asked: what is the message of this book for the 21st century?

One way to answer that question is to apply a set of rules to your reading and interpreting of scripture. Those rules can be expressed through a simple acronym, C O M B –

**CONTEXT** *WHOLE PART-WHOLE*

All scripture must be read and studied in context. It is perilous to pluck a passage out of context. Every passage must first be understood within the framework, *first* of the chapter in which it is found; *then* of the place of that chapter within the book being studied; *then* of the place of that book in the Bible.

Compare Proverbs 22:29 with Ecclesiastes 9:11

> *"Do you see a man skilled in his work? He will stand before kings; He will not stand before obscure men."*

Compared with:

> *"I again saw under the sun that the race is not to the swift and the battle is not to the warriors, and neither is bread to the wise nor wealth to the discerning nor favor to men of ability; for time and chance overtake them all."*

Such promises are like the "law" or promise of sowing and reaping; many things can affect them. There are, of course, other promises that *are* absolute within the larger context of the whole Bible, such as the promise of salvation.

> *"...so that by two unchangeable things in which it is impossible for God to lie, we who have taken refuge would have strong encouragement to take hold of the hope set before us."* (Hebrews 6:18)

So a sound principle of good Hermeneutics and of good Bible study in general is the *"whole - part - whole"* method: that is, study the whole, then the part, then the whole again.

Another sound rule is this; *"let scripture interpret scripture"* - that is, no part of the Bible can be interpreted in a way that contradicts the message of the whole Bible (This is a characteristic fault of many cults).

Perhaps the student can suggest other scriptures that have been plucked out of context, and are used to support false doctrine.

## OTHER SCRIPTURES

Each promise is powerful only in its proper time and place; each promise is conditioned by its own environment, the people to whom it was first spoken; etc.

Each scripture must be compared with **other** scriptures. No text can be properly used in isolation from the testimony of the whole Bible. For example, in Jesus' wilderness temptation, notice how the devil quoted a scripture, which Jesus then countered with another scripture; thus showing that texts cannot be read in isolation, but only within the context of the entire Bible. Specifically, two principles must be remembered:

- The whole Bible is unified around Christ.

    *"Then beginning with Moses and with all the prophets, He explained to them the things concerning Himself in all the Scriptures." (Luke 24:27)*

    *Then I fell at his feet to worship him. But he \*said to me, "Do not do that; I am a fellow servant of yours and your brethren who hold the testimony of Jesus; worship God. For the testimony of Jesus is the spirit of prophecy." (Revelation 19:10)*

- The principle of **progressive revelation** must be recognized; many early ideas are supplanted or changed by later teaching: there is ethical and spiritual progression as biblical revelation unfolds.

    i.e. The admission of the Gentiles to the covenant.

It is a sound principle of hermeneutics therefore, that the gospel must interpret the Law; and the letters (epistles) must interpret the gospel; and so on. Two essential tools for comparing various passages are a **word concordance** and a **topical concordance**. These tools will be discussed in the chapter on study tools.

##  MEANING

There are three levels of meaning in any Biblical passage:

- the meaning intended by the original author

- the meaning his words gain from the larger context of scripture

- the meaning intended for the reader (you) by the Holy Spirit at the time you are reading.

The passage has not been properly understood until all three of these levels have been mastered.

A good place to gain clearer understanding of scriptural meaning is by doing word studies using a good English dictionary, plus Hebrew and Greek word books. It is important, however, to remember that words have different meanings in different contexts: such as prose, poetry, colloquial speech, parable, proverbs, similes, songs, stories, etc.

Metaphors must be treated with care: i.e. such English expressions as *you are a pig; he put his foot in it; walking on air; don't lose your head over it; a bee in his bonnet; bats in the belfry; we're breaking our necks to finish it;* and many more are examples of metaphors that do not mean what they say.

There are a number of ways that words can be studied. They can be studied:

- **Etymologically**, that is, in their root meaning. Care must be taken here however, as a brief check through an English dictionary will show how a word may cease to have any connection with its root.

  Some examples are:

- *fool* comes from the Latin *follis* = a bellows; hence a wind-bag
- *lady* comes from the Latin root meaning *a sacrificial cake*
- *dollar* comes from the German *thaler,* a coin worth about 3 marks
- *focus* comes from the Latin root meaning *joyful*
- *amazed* comes from the Norwegian word meaning *bewildered*
- *gaudy* comes form the Latin root meaning *joyful*

Thus, it is important what meaning is given to a specific word, to insure that a proper translation is given.

- **Comparatively**

Words may be used with a certain amount of flexibility, such as the uses of "law" and "flesh" in the New Testament. Comparing words within their context helps in discovering their meaning.

- **Theologically**

Many words have special meaning theologically. Examples are *Agape* and *Hades.*

- **Background**

What did the passage mean to the original author and reader; what is its historical and cultural setting. For example, one might consider for a moment *"The Song of Solomon".* Many will attempt to interpret this disturbing (for staunch literalists and fundamentalists) in a purely spiritual way, without recognizing its cultural context. First determine the meaning of a word or passage, never a complete book of the bible, in light of its meaning to the writer and readers of the day. This is the only valid starting point for all interpretation, and must remain the checkpoint for all other levels of interpretation.

# REVIEW FOR CHAPTER III

1. What is the study of hermeneutics?

   *INTERPRETATION & EXPLAINATION*

2. In what ways can the Bible be misunderstood?

   1. *HISTORICALLY*
   2. *CULTURALLY*
   3. *LINGUISTICALLY*
   4. *PHILOSOPHICALLY*
   5. *SPIRITUALLY*

   *WRONG PRINCIPALS OF INTERPRETATION*

3. What does the author mean by "COMB" through the Bible?

   *CONTEXT*
   *OTHER SCRIPTURES*
   *MEANING*
   *BACKGROUND*

4. What is meant by "progressive revelation?"

   *OLD IS NEW CONCEALED, NEW IS OLD REVEALED*

5. What is the science of etymology?

   *ROOT MEANING OF A WORD FROM ITS ORIGINS*

6. What are the five ways the present day reader is separated from the writers of the Bible?

*LISTED UNDER QUESTION #2*

7. Record below any personal observations or insights gained through the reading of Chapter III.

*GOOD REFRESHERS*
*LIKED "COMB" ACRONYM*

## CHAPTER IV:

# SOME TIPS ON BIBLE STUDY

*"...that in us you may learn not to exceed what is written,"*

Paul says in 1 Corinthians 4:6. That must be the rule that controls all of our approach to reading and interpreting the Bible.

Although more will be said about various methods of study in a later part of this book, the following should be noted with regards to the study of God's precious word.

## ENCOUNTERING THE WORD OF GOD

The Word of God cannot be truly understood until a sequence of events has taken place. First, the Word must have been written, and then recognized by the church. The Bible must be accepted with a sure belief that it is the Word of God given through and to man by the inspiration of the Holy Spirit. There is no room for an attitude of neutrality in regards to this. It is impossible to establish a relationship with anyone by doubting their veracity. People who are suspicious of everyone they meet are paranoiac and removed by choice from others. Society depends upon trusting people until they are proven untrustworthy.

Someone may ask, what about atheists like C.S. Lewis, who have been converted while trying to mock scripture? They are exceptions of grace. Most unbelievers are confirmed in their unbelief by the Bible, just as most persecutors (unlike Saul) are confirmed in their violence by persecution.

A natural corollary to our trust in the divine origin of scripture is confidence that the Bible was written to be understood by ordinary people. Some highly educated theologians have created more problems than they have solved through their unique and often convoluted interpretation of scripture.

This is not to say that the serious student of the Word of God is not expected, nor should be unwilling, to study the word of God with intense diligence. Sadly, many refuse to apply themselves to the task, preferring a simple Bible, void of complexities, or simply accepting what is stated across pulpits or provided on the internet.

Next, what has been written must be explained so that it is historically understood. That is to say it must be understood in the same way as it was by its first authors and readers. God had to speak to those people in terms that were meaningful to them, just as he has to do in our own time. This task is called *exegesis* = "to ascertain the meaning" of something (from the Greek word that means "to guide someone out of a complexity").

The process of exegesis must be done as much as is possible free from the influences of present pressures, needs, or prejudices, otherwise what will result will not be *exegesis* so much as *eisegesis* = "to introduce one's own (faulty) ideas".

Once the meaning has been established it must be expounded upon. An attempt must be made to determine the doctrines and principles that are being taught, which have universal significance. An example of this is the 23rd Psalm, which is a treatise on ancient shepherding practices. At the same time it teaches us something about the unchanging character of God, his love and guidance of his people, while providing precious promises of his loving care. Our task is not to exclude one meaning from the other, but to first embrace the meaning found within the culture of the day. Then we are to extrapolate into our present time truth which is priceless and timeless.

Sound exposition of scripture requires the formulation of certain reliable rules of interpretation, rules that can be consistently applied to the whole of sacred writing. This is the task of Hermeneutics.

Finally, the scripture must be applied (once discovered and

revealed) to the particular time, place, and circumstance in which the reader finds themselves. In other words, the reader must ask, "What is this passage saying to me right now, in my personal need? What promise does it convey to me? What command does it lay upon me? What challenge does it present to me? How does the Holy Spirit want my life to be influenced today by the Word of God I have discovered?"

This is the special, though not exclusive, task of preaching. It places high importance upon the pastor's function as a teacher, in contrast, with both the Roman Catholic Church, where the priest's role is primarily sacramental; and with much of modern Protestantism, where the pastor's role has become one of counselor and administrator.

**It is only when the five steps given above have been completed that scripture takes on its full character. It is worth the effort for the believer to study with these steps in mind. It will lead the student to a deeper understanding and appreciation of the word of God, producing life and fruitfulness.**

## REVIEW FOR CHAPTER IV

1. Discuss what the author meant by "Encountering the Word of God", in your own words.

## PERSONAL OBSERVATIONS AND NOTE:

# CHAPTER V:

# BIBLE STUDY TOOLS

The secret to a job well done is found in having the correct tools for the job. The carpenter, the surgeon, the dentist, the auto mechanic, ad infinitum all depend on the right tools in order to do a proper job. Not only are the right tools needed, a thorough working knowledge of how to use them is also essential.

For the most part, man's knowledge of the universe is in direct relation to the tools he has and his skill at using those tools. For much of the history of man, those who studied the heavens could number the stars in the sky. With the invention of the telescope, man's knowledge of the stars increased many fold. With each new tool that is developed (more powerful electronic telescopes, etc.) there has come a change in the concepts that man has regarding the universe.

Tools are not meant to take the place of the human mind or skill of the craftsman, but are intended to increase man's ability, whether it is in woodworking or study of the Word of God.

None of the tools of study that are discussed in this chapter are in any way to be thought of as being a substitute for the presence and work of the Holy Spirit. The Holy Spirit has the responsibility, given by the Father and Son of bringing remembrance to our minds of everything that Jesus taught.

> *"But when He, the Spirit of truth, comes, He will guide you into all the truth; for He will not speak on His own initiative, but whatever He hears, He will speak; and He will disclose to you what is to come." (John 16:13)*

The tools presented in this chapter are intended to assist the student in their study of the word. They must never become a substitute for the Bible itself. Two problems noted in students of the Bible are that either they will completely reject the use of any sources outside the Bible or they will rely almost completely on books about Christianity and Christ instead of studying the Book itself. Both tools and the Holy Spirit are necessary for proper understanding; we need the tools, to help us understand the word...but we need to start by simply reading the word, and enjoying our relationship with the Lord.

This chapter presents eight essential tools effective for Bible study. There are many other Bible helps that are available, some of which are listed in a special Bibliography at the end of this book for the student who wishes to expand his or her library beyond the essentials.

## EIGHT ESSENTIAL TOOLS

Most ministers develop fairly extensive libraries over their lifetime. A real love of books seems to be a general characteristic of most preachers. Without question, the minister of the word of God should become acquainted with many types of literature, not in place of good books on theology, but in addition to a Christian library. Some of a preacher's best illustrations will come from literature that is not specifically Christian in nature, such as poetry, or even the newspaper.

It is the purpose of this chapter, however, to present some of the books that are most helpful to the new Bible student. A veteran preacher may also find this information interesting and informative as a review or for teaching purposes.

It is particularly important that the new Bible student (especially a new convert) utilize the simple tools that are presented here rather than becoming "bogged down" with complicated commentaries, or textbooks on theology.

The books listed here are not, except for the first one, listed in any order of importance as a study help. Each book has something special and specific to offer to make Bible study more effective.

## 1. THE BIBLE

As already noted, there is no substitute for the Bible itself. Actually, the serious student of the Word should have not just one, but several different versions or translations of the Bible. Although there are many people who feel that it almost sacrilege to even suggest the usage of anything but the King James Bible, there are a number of versions that do greater justice to the original text.

The King James Bible (KJV) remains to most bible students the most beautiful text because of the poetic quality of the King James English. Some of the words in this translation have become archaic and no longer mean what they used to mean. An example of this archaic language is seen in II Thessalonians. 2:7,

> *"For the mystery of iniquity doth already work: only he who now letteth will let, until he be taken out of the way."*

The word *letteth* (a form of let) means hinders or prevents.

In I Thessalonians 4:15 we see the word *prevent* means *shall not go before*, whereas, in modern English it means to *stop something from happening.* Because the King James Bible has been around for such a long time, most of the people who still use it have few problems with these ancient words. The new convert or young Bible student may have some difficulties with the changed meanings, thus a more modern translation is usually recommended.

The King James Bible should be a part of the student's library of helps, but in addition it is advisable to add the New International Version (NIV), which is thought to be one of the very best available at this time. Further, the Living Letters Version is in the opinion of many a valuable reference tool.

The Living Bible and The Message are written in modern English much like the English spoken in everyday America. Comparing a verse or a portion of scripture from the NIV or the KJV with the same text in the Living Bible often helps to add meaning to the scripture.

The writers' personal favorite is the New American Standard Bible, as it is highly accurate to the original texts, as is an emerging favorite, the English Standard Version.

There are many other versions available that Bible scholars enjoy using in their study. Some of these versions will be listed in the special bibliography. There are also many excellent books on the market that have published side by side versions, so that the student can make many comparisons for a consensus.

Other things that the student should take into consideration about the particular Bible that they choose to use for study are;

- The size of the Bible. It is unwise for the student to use a family style Bible. This might be fine for the home, but is impractical as a Bible to carry on a regular basis.

- When buying a new Bible for the purpose of study, it is important to make sure that it is not loaded with unnecessary pages. Pages used to keep family records, genealogies, etc. only add bulk and weight to the Bible and are not advisable for the Bible that one carries to church.

  With modern technology, fewer and fewer parishioners carry anything more than a Mobile device such as an IPhone or IPAD with various bibles, commentaries, etc. on them.

It is also good to have a Bible concordance in the Bible you study from so that scriptures can be found at times when the student is not at home. Most good Bibles have helpful introductions to books, center column references, etc. that can be valuable. One such Bible that has many useful helps is the Thompson Chain Reference

Bible. One effective feature of the Thompson Chain Reference Bible is the way that it helps the student follow like a chain, topics and themes throughout the Word.

The center column references in many Bibles can help the student quickly find other scripture texts that are related to the one being read. This will increase understanding and reduce the possibility of misinterpreting a passage by taking it out of context.

For example, I Thessalonians 3:3 states,

> *"so that no one would be disturbed by these afflictions; for you yourselves know that we have been destined for this."*

The center column in many Bibles will list a cross-reference to Ephesians 3:13 (among others), which states;

> *"Therefore I ask you not to lose heart at my tribulations on your behalf, for they are your glory."*

This cross-reference enables the student to have greater understanding of what they are studying.

Another excellent Bible that warrants mention is the Open Bible. Both the Open Bible and the Thompson Chain use the King James as well as several other translations. The important thing for the student to remember is, becoming comfortable with a specific bible, though not solely dependent on it, is the goal, and helps facilitate healthy and productive study.

## A WORD ABOUT MARKING THE BIBLE

Many Bible scholars find it very helpful to use either a highlighter pen or a regular ball point pen to mark various verses in their Bibles. It is helpful to highlight or underline certain outstanding scriptures making them easier to find in a hurry, but there are a few cautions to consider. If the student marks too many scriptures the whole purpose of highlighting is defeated. Care must be taken in using a ballpoint that the verses around the one being marked do not become covered and therefore unreadable.

Many students use different colored highlighters to indicate different topics, i.e. red is used to highlight scriptures about salvation (red for the Blood of Christ). If this system is used the student needs to be sure they are consistent in the use of colors so they won't become confused later. The safest method is to create a legend in the front or back of the Bible telling what each color stands for. Also, a wet highlighter may show through the page, so again, caution is required. Dry highlighters are best.

## 2. HALLEY'S BIBLE HANDBOOK

There can be no doubt that _Halley's Bible Handbook_ is and has been one of the most helpful aids to Bible students ever published. Halley's is not a commentary as such, but there is valuable information about every book in the Bible as well as useful information about people, places and customs of the time. The chapter by chapter summary of each of the books of the Bible can be most helpful to the student when looking for specific information on a particular passage of scripture. This valuable tool also tells of important archeological findings that assist in confirming Biblical accuracy.

_Halley's Bible Handbook_ is not intended for the seasoned scholar; however, many veteran preachers use it from time to time to refresh their memory about certain facts. Many pastors will wear out several copies during their lifetime.

## 3. SMITH'S BIBLE DICTIONARY

_Smith's Bible Dictionary_ has earned a reputation as one of the most incisive tools for the Bible student. It describes the important people and places of the Bible, as well as the major teachings of Scripture. The latest edition has a section containing 4000 questions and answers that can be a valuable tool in developing topical Bible Study programs.

Another excellent dictionary is *Unger's Bible Dictionary*, by Merrill F. Unger. Serious Bible scholars often prefer this over Smith's. No Bible student's library would be complete without one of these important reference books.

## 4. A BIBLE CONCORDANCE

A **complete** Bible concordance can be of greater value than one might think. The complete concordance has every word that is in the Bible (yes, even the articles *the, a, an, etc.*) Not only does a complete concordance contain every word that is in the Bible, it will list each place that the word is used. The proper pronunciation of the Hebrew and Greek word are given as well as a reference, along with any roots of that particular word.

Probably the most valuable part of the complete concordance is that each word is given a number that refers to either the Hebrew or the Greek dictionary in the back of the book. By looking up the number in the dictionary the student is able to find the generally accepted original meaning of the word. Next to spending several years studying Greek and Hebrew, this is the best way to discover original meanings.

It is important to purchase a concordance in the same version of the bible being used by the student. If the student is going to use the King James version, he should obtain a concordance for the King James version.

The most popular complete concordance is *Strong's Exhaustive Concordance*. This fine book is often offered on sale and can be purchased for as much as 50% off the retail price. With advances in technology, this tool is now available in electronic format.

## Strong's Exhaustive Concordance of the Bible

## Sample Entry

For purposes of illustration, here are some sample references from the Strong's Exhaustive Concordance, which will show how helpful a tool it can be.

> **Love--** See also loved; love's; loves; lovest; loveth; loving. Ge. 27: 4 make me savory meat, such as I *l'.* (Strong's Number 157) 29:20 few days for the *l'* he had to her. (Strong's Number 160)

> (New Testament)

> Matt. 6:5 for they *l'* to pray standing in the... (Strong's Number 5358)

In the first entry the word *love* is the Hebrew word *ahab.* By looking in the Hebrew and Chaldee Dictionary at the back of Strong's and looking up the Strong's number 157 the student will find:

> 157. (first the Hebrew letters) followed by the English equivalent = ahab then the phonetic pronunciation *aw-hab'* which comes from a prim. root: *to have affection for,* (sexual or otherwise) the word can be translated as *love, like, or friend.*

The New Testament entry in Matthew (Matt.), the Strong's number is 5368. By looking up that number in the Greek Dictionary the student will find:

> 5368. efilew phileo, *fil-eh'-o* from 5384; *to be a friend to (fond of [an individual or an object]),* i.e. *have affection for* (denoting *personal* attachment, as a matter of sentiment...)

The entry 5368 goes on to an even more detailed definition of the word *love* than was noted in Matthew 6:8. It is not difficult to see how valuable this tool would be in serious Bible study. Using the Hebrew and Chaldee Dictionary as well as the Greek Dictionary is not intended to be a complete research of Hebrew or Greek works. There are other tools that will serve the student better here, such as various Lexicons.

Most preachers would feel lost without a concordance. Being able to check the original meanings of words is very important in a day when there are so many different translations of the Bible. Without being a Hebrew or Greek scholar, the average student is able to check for contradictions, etc. in various translations.

The shorter concordance that is found in the back of many bibles serves only to help find a particular verse when away from home. *Strong's Exhaustive Concordance of the Bible* or *Young's Analytical Concordance* is not very practical for carrying to church. The volume is large and quite heavy. It is strictly a library reference source, but one which is most valuable.

**The Treasury of Scripture Knowledge** is another marvelous resource. The Thompson Chain, though a fine tool, is a mere shadow by comparison. As the name indicates, the "Treasury" allows the student to happily review scripture after scripture, taking you from Genesis to Revelation on the hundreds of themes found in scripture. No study library should be without this excellent tool.

## 5. A BIBLE COMMENTARY

There are many different Bible commentaries on the market and four primary types of commentaries - *critical, exegetical, expository, and devotional.* There is a need to discern if a commentary is evangelical or liberal, Protestant or Catholic. Having a substantial collection of all of them on one's shelves and computer is necessary for effective study.

Again, there are many different types of commentaries. For instance, *The Pulpit Commentary* consists of 23 volumes and is a very fine commentary. It costs about $170.00, but it is usually on sale somewhere for about 50 - 60% off. The new Bible student, however, would be best served by beginning with a one volume commentary such as the *Matthew Henry's Commentary*, published by Zondervan Publishing Company. This commentary has been edited down from the original 6 volume version and is quite popular among students. There are several other single volume commentaries available, and having several helps when making comparisons leading to richer study.

The value of a good commentary is especially important when the student looks up a passage of scripture that may be difficult to understand. A commentary allows the student to draw from the scholarship of the writer, which can be a blessing indeed. However, the student must remember that the commentary is not to be considered inspired. The commentary is the learned opinion of another Bible scholar. As a tool, the commentary can be beneficial, but the student must always seek the inspiration of the Holy Spirit to comprehend and respond to truth. A few other commentaries will be listed in the Bibliography at the end of this chapter.

## 6. VINE'S GREEK WORD STUDY

Another valuable tool for the serious Bible student is the *Vine's Greek Word Study*. This fine book lists in alphabetical order some of the more important words in the New Testament and lists the various Greek words from which they came. Under the listing *love* the student will find major Greek words that are translated *love* in the New Testament: *Phileo; agape*. These two words are almost always translated *love* but they each represent a different kind of love. The first word is *Phileo*, which is a love like a brother may have for his brother. *Agape* love is more like the love of God. There are other words that are usually translated as *love*, and it is important for the Bible scholar to be aware of which Greek word was translated to arrive at the correct meaning from a given text.

## 7. A BIBLE ATLAS

Many Bibles have a few maps in the back, but there is often a need for a greater knowledge of the geographical places that are mentioned in the scriptures. Just looking at a map is not enough. The written text in a good Bible atlas will help the student trace the missionary journeys of Paul the Apostle, examine where Jesus ministered, see more clearly the distance that the Hebrews traveled from Egypt to the Promised Land and gain a better knowledge of the famous places discussed in the Bible.

Any Bible bookstore will carry several different Bible Atlases. The student should examine several and choose the one that seems to be most interesting and is within the student's budget. Some students find it helpful to purchase larger wall maps to hang in their study so that they can refer to them as they are studying.

## 8. COMPUTER SOFTWARE

For the student who has a computer, there are a number of good Bible programs available. These software programs will do everything that can be done with the concordance and more. The programs have anywhere from one to eight different translations of the Bible with a complete Hebrew and Greek dictionary. Depending on the particular program that the student uses, it is possible to compare verses from several different translations at the same time. With a good printer, the student can print out any scripture from the Bible for use in sermon outlines or reports.

Probably the most comprehensive software program (though there is a learning curve to use it well) is the Logos Software (see more on this in the bibliography) and for ease of usage for the beginning student, eSword is highly recommended, as a free software that is quite user friendly and adequate for most study circumstances.

Bible software programs are advertised in most Christian magazines and can be frequently found in the larger Bible bookstores or online.

# BIBLIOGRAPHY OF OTHER BOOKS

The following list of books is not exhaustive. It represents some of the better study reference materials that will help the Bible student develop a well rounded education. Additional books and materials will be listed in the whole text Bibliography at the end of this book.

Cruden, Alexander. *Cruden's Complete Concordance.*

Edersheim, Alfred. *The Life and Times of Jesus The Messiah.*

Hastings, James. *A Dictionary of the Bible.* one volume

Hastings, James *A Dictionary of the Bible.* five volumes

Henry, Matthew. *Matthew Henry's Commentary on the Whole Bible.* six volumes

Lightfoot, J. *A Commentary on the New Testament from the Talmud and Hebraica.* 4 volumes

Matthews, V.H. *Manners and Customs in the Bible.*

Nave, O. *Nave's Topical Bible.* This would be the book to buy first after the main tools listed above. This volume lists scripture under various topics. By looking under the topic *Anger* the student would find many scriptures (written out) that deal with the topic.

Sheldon, H.C. *History of the Christian Church.* 5 volumes

Vincent, M.R. *Vincent's Word Studies in the New Testament.* 4 volumes

Wilson, W, *Wilson's Old Testament Word Studies.*

Young, R. *Young's Analytical Concordance to the Bible.*

The Bible student should develop the habit of inquiring of pastor friends and other Bible scholars about the books that they have found to be particularly helpful.

All of the books discussed in this chapter are more or less reference works. There are many books that are not reference books that will make a valuable addition to the serious student's library. It is profitable for a Bible student to spend time occasionally just browsing in a Bible bookstore.

## Some Final Thoughts from Dr. Ken Chant

"I liked your recommendation that pastors/Bible scholars should read more widely than just theological works. That could hardly be more true!

Wonderful riches can be gleaned from philosophy, fiction, biographies, histories, mythology, etc. Poetry should be included, too, for nothing else can reveal the human condition quite so powerfully as great poetry. It has been said, and I almost agree, that a person who fails to read poetry is only half human! Which may be why more than a third of the Bible is poetry.

Two free software programs are the Online Bible (OLB), and E-sword (referenced above). Both of them come with an array of free reference materials, with scores more books available at a reasonable price. Word Search is another piece of excellent Bible software. It is not free, but includes a vast array of translations, commentaries, reference tools, etc. There is also the Bible Analyzer, which is free. It has a different collection of additional materials. I use them all. Between them, they probably add at least 500 books to my library."

Thanks Dr. Chant…well stated as always!

The next chapter will deal with some study aids other than books. Some suggestions will be made about various methods of study, and the student will be introduced to a number of study guide sheets that can be of help in the study of God's Word.

## REVIEW FOR CHAPTER V

1. List the Bible tool(s) you have in your library at this time?

2. How can each of the Bible tools assist the student in their studies?
   - Bible
   - Halley's Bible Handbook
   - Smith's Bible Dictionary
   - A Bible Concordance
   - A Bible Commentary
   - Vine's Greek Word Study
   - A Bible Atlas

3. What other Bible tools have you found to be helpful in your studies?

4. Provide your personal comments as desired on this Chapter below.

# CHAPTER VI:

# SOME MODELS OF STUDY AND STUDY AIDS

There are many different methods of study. The student will find that from time to time he will change his study methods, if for no other reason than to avoid boredom. There are times when one particular method is better because of a desired outcome. There will be times when it is advisable to study an entire book of the Bible at one time, while at other times a chapter study will be in order. A topical or thematic study can be fun and profitable, while at other times the student will want to do a word study. Each of these methods are discussed briefly in this chapter.

## BIBLE STUDY MODELS

Regardless of the method that the student uses they should always have a personal time for devotional reading. Many Christians prefer to read the Bible through from Genesis to Revelation as a part of this devotional time. Others desire to spend time in those parts of the Bible that tend towards the inspirational or poetic, such as are found in the Psalms or Proverbs. This method of selective reading presents the danger of neglecting important portions of scripture, which can be just as inspirational, and at times infinitely more profitable to ones spiritual growth. The Lord desires to inspire his children, and also to correct, rebuke and encourage as needed. Only the Holy Spirit knows our true need at any given time.

Thus, let us look at some of the formal forms of Bible study, while leaving devotional reading for another time.

## 1. WHOLE BOOK STUDY

The Whole Book Study method is a type of study that attempts to determine everything possible about:

- The author of a given Bible book
- The time frame in which the book was written
- The people to whom the book was written
- The reason why the book was written
- What the major problems were at the time of the writing
- What key verses can be found within the confines of the book
- What central meaning can be revealed for today

After answering these major questions the student should outline the entire book. An outline guide will be found in the appendix of this book. There are also sample study guides for Chapter Study; Verse Study; Bible Character Study; Word Study and Topic Study. (For more on this, see Dr. DeKoven's *Journey Through the Old Testament* and *Journey Through the New Testament).*

The student may wish to copy these pages from the text and duplicate them for his/her personal use. One excellent method of keeping these guides for further reference is to place them in a three ring binder using tab dividers to separate the different types of guides. It is advisable to file the guides in alphabetical order so that they can be easily retrieved in the future. Over the years the student will accumulate a rich source of material that can be used in the preparation of sermons, teachings and written articles.

In addition to the study guides there is a sample reference sheet that can be used with the standard guides. This reference sheet is intended for the recording of illustrations, examples and facts from sources other than the Bible. By stapling the reference sheet to the study guide, the student will have another rich source of information for preparing sermons, etc.

Not every book of the Bible needs to be studied in the same way. Some books can just be read without using the Book Study Guide. The Student will discover that the New Testament books will fast become favorite books to study. However, many of the Old Testament books are also rich in teaching, especially as a foundation for New Testament truths. The student must not neglect Old Testament studies.

One of the most important elements in studying a whole book is to watch for those verses that are a promise or a fulfillment of a promise found elsewhere in the Bible. For example, the book of Isaiah is rich in prophecies and promises regarding the coming Messiah. There can be no doubt of the importance of the relationship of Isaiah 61:1-2 and Luke 4:18-19.

Isaiah 61:1-3 (written about 700 years before the birth of Jesus) reads,

> *"The Spirit of the Lord God is upon me, because the Lord has anointed me to bring good news to the afflicted; He has sent me to bind up the brokenhearted, to proclaim liberty to captives and freedom to prisoners; to proclaim the favorable year of the Lord and the day of vengeance of our God; to comfort all who mourn.*

Luke 4:18-19 (Jesus is in the temple at about 30 years of age. He stands and reads to the assembled elders).

> *"The Spirit of the Lord is upon me, because He anointed me to preach the gospel to the poor. He has sent me to proclaim release to the captives, and recovery of sight to the blind, to set free those who are oppressed, to proclaim the favorable year of the Lord."*

The following is a suggested sequence that a beginning student may wish to follow:

| Old Testament | New Testament |
|---|---|
| Isaiah | Gospel of John |
| Psalms | I John |
| Proverbs | Ephesians |
| Joel | Acts |
| Joshua | Mark |
| Judges | I Timothy |

By the time the student is finished with the above mentioned books, he/she should have a fair idea of where they would like to go next. It should be noted here that if the student is taking other Bible College courses, they should feel free to study, say the book of Acts, while taking a course on the Acts of the Apostles.

## 2. CHAPTER STUDY GUIDE

The Chapter Study method involves an intense examination of one of the chapters of one of the books of the Bible. It is advisable that the chapter studied be from one of the books of the Bible that has already been studied and outlined. The reason this approach is advisable is that it is always better to concentrate on one book for a while rather than skip from book to book. This properly follows the important learning axiom of repetition.

Again, not every chapter of every book will lend itself to the type of study suggested by the study guides. Some chapters need to be read over carefully several times to make sure that something important is not being missed. The student should begin every chapter study by reading over the chapter two or three times before deciding on whether or not to use a guide sheet.

While studying a chapter, it is important to look for key verses. Some of those key verses should be highlighted so that the student can find them more easily later on. Remember, some of the most important questions to ask while doing a chapter study include, "What did the passage mean within the cultural context of the days of the writer?" and "What does this chapter have to say to me?"

Some of the best chapters of the Bible with which to start are listed below. They are only suggestions, but, are suggested because they are either very inspirational, contain important teaching, or provide important warnings that every Christian needs to hear:

| Book | Chapter |
|------|---------|
| John | 3 |
| Psalms | 1 |
| Psalms | 23 |
| Ephesians | 4/5 |
| Galatians | 5 |
| Romans | 6 |
| Acts | 2-3 |
| Proverbs | 3 |

It is recommended that the student take time to tackle at least one of the chapters listed above, and see where the Lord leads.

## 3. VERSE STUDY

Many verses in the Bible contain so much truth that they demand a careful study all by themselves. A popular verse that serves as an example is John 3:16.

> *"For God so loved the world, that He gave His only begotten Son, that whoever believes in Him shall not perish, but have eternal life."*

The Word Study Guide will help the student in finding:

**The Key word(s)**

**The Main thought(s)**

**How the verse appears in other translations**

**The main thought in relation to other verses in the Bible**

In the section entitled **Other Observations** the student should make a note of whether the verse is one that should be memorized. If the verse is to be memorized, the student should make a memorization card at the time he is studying the verse. Sample Memory Cards are provided in the section on Memorization.

## 4. WORD STUDY

A Word study can be exciting indeed. Just the study of the word *love* will result in many new truths that will prove highly profitable and inspirational. In the Gospel of John, chapter 21, Jesus has an interesting conversation with Peter. The conversation does not make much sense until the student examines the different Greek words that are all translated *love*. (The student might want to take time to look up the words in their Strong´s or similar concordance).

As another example, there are over 200 scriptures in the Bible with the word *anger*. There are more than a dozen definitions.

Word Study is one method of study that highly depends on reference sources other than the Bible. The *Strong's* concordance is one primary source. When using the Word Study Guide it is important to note the Strong's number for a particular definition to avoid the necessity of looking the word up again later.

A second source, as noted previously, for word study is *Vine's Expository Dictionary of New Testament Words* by William E. Vine. The usage of this book has already been described above.

Although a modern English dictionary is not listed in the primary tools for Bible Study, it is an excellent (really, vital) source for word study. Many Bible scholars consult the *Webster's Complete*

_Dictionary_ first, in doing a word study.

## 5. BIBLE CHARACTER STUDY

Many students will find the study of Bible characters most fascinating. It is always interesting to ask, "Why did this person wind up being a part of such an important document as the Bible?" Sadly, many of them are mentioned in the Bible because of their infamous deeds, such as Judas Iscariot, whose end was more than tragic. But what is really known about Judas besides the fact that he betrayed the Lord? It seems a pity that most Christians know little more than that he was the great betrayer. Is he mentioned anywhere else in the Bible? Is there any hope for his final salvation? (Sorry, no answers provided here, only questions. **You** do the research!)

Others, like Paul the Apostle are interesting because their life before and after they had an encounter with Jesus is described. Paul makes such an interesting study that it is recommended that the new student begin with him. The Bible Character Study Guide is very helpful in this kind of study.

## 6. TOPIC STUDY

The _Thompson's Chain Reference Bible, Treasury of Scripture Knowledge_ and _Nave's Topical Bible,_ are sources that will prove invaluable in conducting a topic study. The topic study is just what the name implies. The student selects a topic and proceeds to search through the Bible, reviewing the various verses that discuss that topic. In doing a topical study, it is wise to limit the scope of the topic to be studied. To select the _Holy Spirit_ as a topic would send the student into so many directions as to make profitable study nearly impossible.

For example, _The Holy Spirit_ as a topic can be broken down into many sub-topics: _The Comforter, Symbols of the Holy Spirit, The Baptism in the Holy Spirit, The Gifts of the Holy Spirit, The Fruit of the Holy Spirit,_ etc. The student must be able to narrow (limit) the topic to a reasonable boundary for study to be fruitful.

Topic study is most helpful in the preparation of sermons, teachings, and material for an article to be written. Often during a topic study research, the student will find many ideas for further research. These should always be noted immediately on the Further Research sheet to be kept in the front of the loose leaf notebook.

## REVIEW FOR CHAPTER VI

1. Briefly describe the 6 "Models of Bible Study" found in this chapter.

    1.

    2.

    3.

    4.

    5.

    6.

2. Can you think of any other model?

3. List 5 Bible characters that would be interesting to study.

    1

    2.

    3.

    4.

    5

4. Personal Observations and notes.

## CHAPTER VII:

# OTHER STUDY METHODS

### 1. MEMORIZATION

Memorization does not come easily for most people. It is true that memorizing anything takes a certain amount of work and determination, but the results make the effort worth while.

All of the study that one may do will not take the place of the special words of the Lord that have been hidden in the believer's heart. There are times when the child of God will not have a Bible handy, and there will be many times that one's notes are not readily available. The Word that has been committed to memory will be a true blessing in these situations. Hear the Psalmist words,

> *"Your word I have treasured in my heart, that I may not sin against You." (Psalm 119:11)*

One cannot help but recall what happened to Jesus on the Mount of Temptation. Satan actually quoted scripture, with his own twist, in an attempt to cause Jesus to fall. However, Christ quoted other scriptures that corrected the errors of Satan's arguments. The defense of Christ was, *"It is written..."* (See Matthew 4:1-11). Satan was defeated because of the power of the Word!

Quoting the Word of God is a primary strategy for the believer today to overcome the attacks of Satan.

Being able to quote the scriptures will help the Christian to gain victory in life.

> *"How blessed is the man who does not walk in the counsel of the wicked, nor stand in the path of sinners, nor sit in the seat of scoffers!* ***But his***

*delight is in the law of the LORD, and in His law he meditates day and night. He will be like a tree firmly planted by streams of water, which yields its fruit in its season and its leaf does not wither; and in whatever he does, he prospers." (Psalm 1:1-3)*

Memorizing the Word of God can help the Christian become an effective personal witness. Being able to quote the scriptures that can lead someone to the saving knowledge of Christ will give confidence to the witness as well as minister to the sinner. Searching through the Bible to find scriptures when trying to share Christ with a potential new believer can distract from the task of sharing the Good News of Jesus.

## SOME HELP FOR MEMORIZATION:

One of the most powerful techniques in memorization is *repetition*. Repetition must not be a simple, unconscious repeating of words. A valuable tool that will assist the student in memorizing is the scripture card. Bible bookstores often sell sets of memory cards, but it is better for the student to make up their own set. A 3" X 5" or A5 index card works quite well. Some people prefer a smaller card. If the user is going to write the scriptures in long hand, the larger card makes sense. (See the forms section in the Appendix for an example).

The card should have written at the top the subject that the scripture deals with, i.e. **Salvation, Prayer, Holy Spirit, etc.**

Next, the scripture should be copied onto the card, either typed or handwritten. Care must be taken to copy the scripture exactly as it appears in the Bible. Do not omit any words or punctuation marks.

Finally, the scripture reference should be noted at the bottom of the card. On the reverse side of the card the scripture reference and the topic should be written.

It is better to memorize a few scriptures at a time than to attempt to memorize many scriptures or long passages of scripture. The real key to successful memorization is **repetition and review.** Every scripture that is memorized should be reviewed on a regular basis. Educational psychologists have demonstrated that no matter how well something is learned, most of it will be forgotten over a short period of time unless it is reviewed regularly.

Finally, reciting scripture aloud will facilitate the process of memorization. While reciting aloud, it helps to "picture the verse" being recited. The scripture reference should always be recited with the verse and as much care as possible be given to accuracy in terms of the reference and the verse itself.

### SOME VERSES AND TOPICS TO LEARN

The following list of topics represents a few of the first verses to learn:

### TOPICS

The new birth - God's love for man - Sinfulness of all men - The penalty of Sin- Victory over sin - The new nature - Salvation as a result of Grace - The Peace of God-Victory over sin - Victory over worry - Victory over depression, etc.

### WHERE TO START:

A good place to start is with scripture that is already memorized or almost memorized. A few examples include:

| | | |
|---|---|---|
| **John 3:16** | **I John 1:9** | **Romans 3:23** |
| **Ephesians 1:7** | **Romans 6:23** | **Romans 8:1** |
| **Romans 12:1-2** | **Romans 10:13** | |

More scripture could be added to this list, but it is better for the student to begin adding those which are most meaningful to him or her.

## REVIEW FOR CHAPTER VII

1. Make a list of your own scriptures to memorize.

   •

   •

   •

2. Get together with another Christian and practice using the scriptures you have memorized.

3. Find an unsaved person and ask them to listen to you as you quote scriptures you have memorized. This is a very good evangelistic tool.

4. Tell what happened when you witnessed to an unsaved person.

5. List your personal observations and objections to memorization. How might you overcome your objections?

## CHAPTER VIII:

# SUMMARY

## BECOME AN EFFECTIVE BIBLE STUDENT

It will take time to become an efficient Bible student. Old habits need to be changed, and new habits need to be developed. The student must not become discouraged when failure occurs. The only real failure goes to the person who never attempts in the first place.

The first prerequisite of becoming a good Bible student is determination. In the beginning there will be times when ones study schedule is disrupted. Distractions will come from every possible source. Once the pattern of consistent study habits have been established, it will become easier to manage the distractions of life.

To facilitate positive study habits, the student should decide on the location for study. If at all possible, the study area should be a private room that can be locked. Not everyone will be so fortunate as to have this luxury, in which case a secluded corner of a room that is as void of distracting elements as possible will suffice. The family room where the kids watch television or play throughout the day will not be very conducive to effective study. A quiet bedroom can make an excellent place to study. The important thing is to have a special corner where study materials may be left out without causing marital conflict.

Wherever the location may be, it should be conducive to study. Sufficient lighting is important. A work space such as a desk or table that is large enough to accommodate several books and writing materials at the same time is essential. A typewriter or computer is also helpful in the study process, but there must be adequate room to accommodate them. If equipment must be packed away and unpacked again for each study period, not only will precious time be wasted, but the student will become more apt to simply not use the equipment.

The time of day that an individual studies is more important than the location. The family room may be an excellent place of study, if the study is done in the early morning or late evening. Studying late at night, however, may be rife with other problems due to fatigue or family obligations.

## A SUGGESTED STUDY PLAN

Again, the suggestions in this text are only intended to assist the student get started. As time passes, most students will develop a pattern of study that will best suit them. The following suggested plan represents a minimum study period.

The total time for study is only 40 minutes per day. It is more profitable to study for 40 minutes per day than to spend 3-4 hours at one setting. People tend to learn more effectively in short segments with frequent repetition. The student should understand that the following plan of study only relates to the study of the Bible. If the student is taking other Bible classes or working towards a degree, he/she will need to spend additional study time on the other subjects being taken.

| | |
|---|---|
| **DEVOTIONAL READING** | **15 MINUTES** |
| **BIBLE STUDY** | **15 MINUTES** |
| **RECORDING** | **10 MINUTES** |

Forty minutes per day represents only 1/36 of a day. It may seem like a lot of time, but the fact is that most people find that 40 minutes does not seem like enough time. As the student becomes more efficient in the use of the various study tools, he will be able to do highly productive work in the allotted 40 minutes. One must not become discouraged at first if little seems to be accomplished. Studying is like any other skill. The more it is practiced the greater the efficiency.

It is also important not to become anxious nor feel guilty in the beginning. Guilt will most certainly have one of two results: the student will try to study longer and harder resulting in more frustration, or the student will simply stop studying.

## TIME SAVERS

There are several things that the student can do to use time more effectively. First is the matter of organization, which has already been mentioned. If the student has a relatively quiet place to study, where all of the tools of study can be organized in a way that they will be readily available, he will become much more efficient in his studies. Having to search for a particular book or item not only wastes time, but causes certain frustration and needless delay.

The faithful use of the study guides included with this text will prove to be a time saver. If the guides are filed in an organized manner (such as within a large three ring binder with tabs to partition the book into sections) they will become handy reference materials in themselves.

Another time saver is the use of a good shorthand system. Granted, not many students reading this book are fortunate enough to have learned shorthand in high school. There are other methods of shorthand that can be learned or simply developed by the learner themself.

The medical profession uses many examples of shorthand. The average lay person may not know what they mean, but doctors, nurses and pharmacists understand exactly what the shorthand expression means. For example, the notation on a prescription that reads *b.i.d.* means "two times daily", while *stat means* "immediately." The letter *c* with a line above is used for the word "with" and so forth.

The student can develop a shorthand of his own. Words that are used over and over again can be shortened, such as Holy Spirit becomes H.S. and deliverance can be *del.* It is judicious that the user be consistent in whatever shorthand is used. It is wise to develop a shorthand system slowly, one word at a time, while developing a ledger of what each shorthand notation means.

The advantages of using a shorthand system are that it saves time and space. More can be recorded in a smaller space in less time than by writing everything out.

Whatever you do as a student of the word of God, please do not hesitate to begin. Some study is better than none, and all study with a focus on knowing the Lord Jesus Christ in greater intimacy is of benefit to you and the Body of Christ. So...

## GO FOR IT!

## YOU ARE ENCOURAGED TO GO FORWARD IN THE MOST EXCELLENT PURSUIT OF KNOWING GOD THROUGH HIS WORD...IT IS WORTH EVERY EFFORT,

## FOR TO KNOW THE LORD THROUGH THE KNOWLEDGE OF HIS WORD IS TO KNOW LIFE IN ITS FULLNESS!!!

# BIBLIOGRAPHY

Provided here is a simple bibliography of adult level (age 14 and up) educational resources designed for systematic study of God's Word.

All are available from: **VISION PUBLISHING, 1672 Main Street E109, Ramona, CA 92065 or may be ordered by calling 1-800-9-VISION(984-7466).**

**Or visit our website at <u>www.booksbyvision.com</u>.**

Chant, Ken    *Authenticity and Authority of the Bible*

Chant, Ken. *Christian Life: Patterns of Gracious Living* (How to live)

Chant, Ken. *Dynamic Christian Foundations* (Basic Doctrines of the Faith)

Chant, Ken. *Faith Dynamics* (What Faith is and how to walk in it)

Chant, Ken. *Great Words of the Gospel* (What key Bible words mean)

Chant, Ken. *The Bible* (From ancient manuscripts to modern Bible)

DeKoven, Stan. *40 Days to the Promise: A Way Through the Wilderness* (Keys to the overcoming life)

DeKoven, Stan. *Catch the Vision*

DeKoven, Stan. *Grace and Truth*

DeKoven, Stan. *Journey Through the Old Testament* (Bible Survey)

DeKoven, Stan. *Journey Through the New Testament* (Bible Survey)

DeKoven, Stan. *Journey to Wholeness: Restoration of the Soul (God's Plan for Kingdom living)*

DeKoven, Stan. *Keys to Successful Living*

DeKoven, Stan. *Marriage and Family Life: A Christian Perspective* (God's Plan for the Christian Home)

DeKoven, Stan. *New Beginnings: A Sure Foundation* (Believers First steps)

DeKoven, Stan. *That's the Kingdom of God*

DeKoven, Stan. *Transferring the VISION*

# APPENDIX

## SAMPLE STUDY HELPS

# BOOK STUDY GUIDE

Name of the book studied.

Author of the Book

To whom was it written?

Why was it written?

What were some of the major problems of the day?

What solutions were offered?

What was the main meaning for that day?

What could the meaning be for today?

Key verse(s)


Additional comments (what did you get out of the study?)

# CHAPTER STUDY GUIDE

Book

Chapter

Date

What is the main idea expressed?

What is the Key verse(s)

Is there a main lesson?

Are some warnings given?

Why was it written?

To whom was it written?


Is there something that I should apply to my life?


Other observations:


Further Bible References:

# VERSE STUDY GUIDE

Book_____     Chapter_____

Verse_____      Date _____

Write the verse here…

What are the key words?

Compare the verse with another translation:

What is the main difference?

What is the main thought of the verse?

Are there other verses in the Bible that are similar?

Are there some questions I have about this verse that I need to ask someone about?

# BIBLE CHARACTER STUDY GUIDE

Character's Name:

Main Scripture:

Date of Study:

Time of the character's existence:

Why was this character mentioned in the Bible?

What did you learn from his/her life?

Who were his/her friends or relatives?

What influence did he/she have on others?

Other significant facts you learned about his/her life?

From the Bible:


From other sources:


Personal Observations:

# WORD STUDY GUIDE

Word studied:

Greek or Hebrew Form

Date of Study:

Main Text from which taken:

Other texts where found in this form:

What is the Strong's number?

What is the definition from Strong's?

Other Source(s) consulted:

Definition from other sources:

What is the significance of the definition of the word in the main text?

Other roots from which the word came:

Personal Observations:

# TOPIC STUDY GUIDE

Topic to Study:

Date:

Primary Book, Chapter and Verse:

Sources Used:

Reason for the Study:

Best Scriptures that deal with the topic:

Secondary scripture dealing with the topic:

Difference between the way the topic is dealt with in the Old and New Testaments:

Main lessons learned:

Suggestions for further study:

## OTHER SOURCES

To be filed with:

Book Study:

Character Study:

Chapter Study:

Word Study:

Verse Study:

Topic Study:

Type of material: Article, Illustration, Humorous illustration, Etc.

Source where material was found:

Date of Material:

How does the material relate to the study?

Personal notes about the study:

# FURTHER RESEARCH NOTES

Date:                     Research notes (what to research)


## Books to Buy


| Author | Title | Publisher |
|--------|-------|-----------|
| 1. | | |
| 2. | | |
| 3. | | |
| 4. | | |
| 5. | | |
| 6. | | |
| 7. | | |
| 8. | | |

## SAMPLE MEMORY CARDS

---

**Prayer**

"Hitherto, have ye asked nothing in my name;

ask, and ye shall receive,

that your joy may be full."

**John 16:24**

---

**The reverse side of the 3X5 card looks like this:**

---

**Prayer**

**John 16:24**

---

## About the Author

Stan E. DeKoven, Ph.D., M.F.T is a licensed Marriage, Family and Child Therapist in San Diego, Calif., and a certified School Psychologist.

Dr. DeKoven received his Bachelor's degree in Psychology from San Diego State University, his Masters in Counseling from Webster University, and his Ph.D. in Counseling Psychology from the Professional School of Psychological Studies. He has also completed a Bachelors and Masters in Theology, and his Doctorate in Ministry from Evangelical Theological Seminary. He is Founder and President of Vision International University in Ramona, Calif. and the International Training and Education Network.

Dr, DeKoven is also the publisher and author of over 35 books in practical theology, counseling and leadership, and a conference speaker. He is available to teach and minister on a variety of different topics which you can find listed on his website at www.drstandekoven.com or you may contact him in his office at the address below:

Vision International and ITEN
1115 D Street
Ramona, CA 92065
1 800 – 9 – VISION
www.vision.edu
sdekoven@vision.edu

CPSIA information can be obtained
at www.ICGtesting.com
Printed in the USA
FFOW02n0004150917
39967FF